AI FOR KIDS
LEARN WITH ROBOT TECHIE AND AI SPARKY

A Fun STEM Adventure into Artificial Intelligence for Ages 5-12

Written and Created by
Kristina Gedmintaite

Copyright 2025 Kristina Gedmintaite.
All rights reserved

Dedication

*To my sons, Vladimir and Aleksandr —
Two brilliant young explorers.
You are my greatest inspiration.*

*Keep learning, keep imagining,
and always believe in your dreams.*

CONTENTS

Introduction 5
Meet the Characters 6

Chapter 1. What Is Artificial Intelligence? 9
Chapter 2. How Machines Learn 13
Chapter 3. Robots in Real Life 17
Chapter 4. AI in Everyday Life......................... 20
Chapter 5. Can AI Be Creative?....................... 26
Chapter 6. Can AI Be Wrong? & How AI Sees the World. 30
Chapter 7. The Future of AI........................... 33
Chapter 8. You and AI – What Comes Next? 38

🚀 You're the Future of AI!.......................... 41
🔍 Glossary of AI Terms............................ 43
Note to Parents and Teachers 44

Introduction

Welcome to a journey into the world of Techie and Sparky – two friendly characters designed to guide young minds through the exciting landscape of AI and technology. This book is intended to ignite curiosity, build foundational knowledge, and spark creativity.

Together, we'll explore the basics of artificial intelligence, learn about real-world uses, and meet characters who make learning feel like play. Whether you're a curious kid or a supportive adult, this book offers a window into the future – one page at a time.

Meet the Characters

Techie

Techie is a clever, kind-hearted robot made of smooth white panels and glowing blue lights. With big curious eyes and gentle hands, Techie loves to learn, create, and explain how technology works in the real world.

You'll often find Techie drawing ideas on a tablet, solving problems, or helping Sparky explore something new.

Fun fact: Techie can sketch digital landscapes and explain how computers learn—all at the same time!

Sparky

Sparky is a bright, glowing blue AI orb with sparkling wings and endless energy. He's always learning, asking questions—and sometimes making silly mistakes along the way!

Fun fact: Sparky once tried to teach a microwave to rap. It was... crunchy.

Sparky isn't just fun— he's an AI in training! That means he's still learning how to understand the world, just like you.

With Techie and Sparky by your side, every lesson becomes a story—and every question a new adventure.

Chapter 1:

What Is Artificial Intelligence?

Have you ever wondered how your voice assistant knows what you're saying, or how a robot vacuum knows where to go? That's artificial intelligence — or AI for short.

AI means making computers and machines think, learn, and solve problems, kind of like how people do. But don't worry — they don't have feelings, and they're not building robot armies (at least not anytime soon!).

Let's Ask Techie:

> *"AI is like giving a computer a clever brain! It helps me solve puzzles, talk to humans, and even support Sparky while he's still learning."*

A Quick Look at the Past: How AI Began

Artificial Intelligence might sound super modern — but the idea started a long time ago.

Long, Long Ago...

Even thousands of years ago, people dreamed about creating mechanical beings that could think. Ancient myths talked about talking statues, magical machines, and thinking robots.

💡 The Real Start – 1950s

AI became a real science in the 1950s. A smart mathematician named Alan Turing asked:

"Can machines think?"

He created the Turing Test — a way to check if a machine could behave like a human in conversation.

In 1956, a group of scientists met at a place called Dartmouth College in the USA. They had a big idea:

let's try to build machines that can think! That's when the term "Artificial Intelligence" was born.

🛠 The First AI Programs

In the 1960s and 70s, early AI programs could solve math problems, play chess, or understand simple sentences.

But they were still pretty slow and not very clever.

🚀 Fast Forward to Today

Now, AI is everywhere:

- △ It helps doctors find illnesses faster
- △ It drives cars without drivers
- △ It recommends your favorite songs
- △ It even helps Techie and Spark learn new skills!

💬 Let's Ask Sparky:

"AI is like a robot's magic brain — but instead of spells, it uses data and code!"

🧠 Quiz Time!
(Let's see how much you remember!)

1. **What does AI stand for?**
   a. Amazing Intelligence
   b. Artificial Intelligence
   c. Automatic Invention

2. **Who asked, "Can machines think?" in the 1950s?**
   a. Albert Einstein
   b. Alan Turing
   c. Elon Musk

3. **Which of these is NOT an example of AI today?**
   a. A calculator
   b. A self-driving car
   c. A robot that talks

✅ Quiz Answers:

1. b) Artificial Intelligence
2. b) Alan Turing
3. a) A calculator

Chapter 2:
How Machines Learn

Have you ever played a game so many times that you started getting really good at it? Machines learn in a similar way — by trying, making mistakes, and getting better with practice!

🧠 Learning from Data

Imagine you show a robot 1,000 pictures of cats and 1,000 pictures of dogs. At first, the robot gets confused.

But each time you tell it, "This is a cat!" or "That's a dog!", it learns patterns:

△ Cats often have pointy ears.

△ Dogs have longer noses.

△ Cats meow. Dogs bark.

Eventually, the robot becomes really good at knowing which is which — even with new pictures it's never seen before!

😎 Let's Ask Techie:

"Machines don't learn like humans. They learn from data — numbers, words, pictures — and they find patterns inside!"

🧪 Kinds of Machine Learning

There are three main types of machine learning:

1. **Supervised Learning**

   You give the machine examples with answers.

   Like showing Sparky a banana and saying, "This is a banana."

2. **Unsupersised Learning**

   You give the machine a bunch of stuff and no answers — and it tries to group things on its own!

   Like giving Sparky a box of toys and asking him to sort them however he wants.

3. **Reinforcement Learning**

   The machine learns by trying and getting rewards or penalties.

   Like Sparky playing a maze game — he gets a star for turning the right way, and nothing for the wrong way.

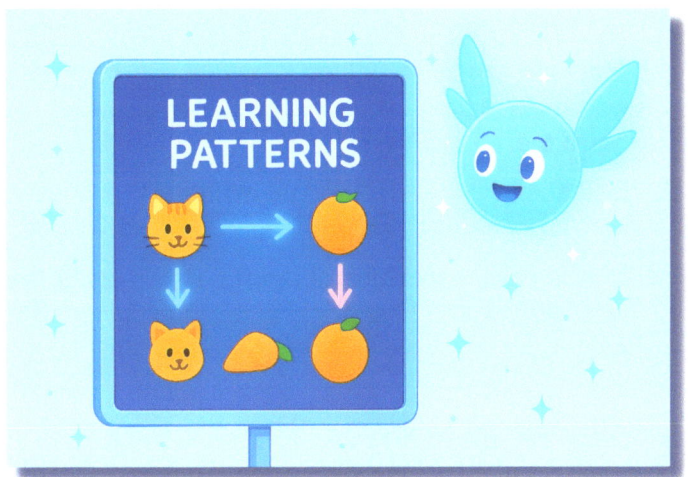

⚡ Sparky's Confession:

"I once thought a pineapple was a type of hedgehog. But thanks to machine learning, I now know better!"

🎯 Real-Life Examples of Machine Learning:

△ Your TV recommends shows you might like? That's machine learning.

△ Your email filters spam automatically? Also machine learning.

△ A car that can drive by itself? Yup — it learned by watching thousands of hours of driving data!

💡 Did You Know?

- Machine learning helped a computer beat the world champion at the chess game, which is quite a difficult task!
- Some AIs can write songs, make art, and even tell jokes — but they still don't laugh at them.
- If you feed a machine bad data, it can learn the wrong things — like thinking a stop sign is a donut!

🧪 Challenge Activity: "Find the Pattern!"

Can you guess what the AI would learn?

Look at these words:

- 🍎 Apple
- 🍌 Banana
- 🍊 Orange
- 🚗 Car
- 🍇 Grape

Which one doesn't belong? Why?

(Hint: Four are fruits. One is not!)

Chapter 3:
Robots in Real Life

When you hear the word robot, what do you picture? A shiny metal person with blinking eyes?

Well, robots are real — and they're already working all around us!

Some robots look like people, but most look more like machines with arms, wheels, or even wings.

🤖 What Is a Robot?

A robot is a machine that can:

- Sense (see, hear, or feel things)
- Think (process data or instructions)
- Act (move or do something)

Robots can work all by themselves or follow instructions from a person or computer.

When a robot uses AI, it gets even smarter!

⚡ Sparky's Quiz Corner:

"Which of these is a real robot?"

- A vacuum that cleans your room by itself
- A dog that does backflips
- A toaster that just sits there

✓ Answer: The vacuum! It can sense, think, and act — just like a robot should.

⊕ Where Can We Find Robots?

Robots are working in all kinds of places:

- Hospitals: Some robots help with surgery, or bring tools to doctors.
- Factories: Robots build cars, package food, and lift heavy things.
- Homes: There are robots that mop floors, mow lawns, or even tell bedtime stories.

- Space: Robots like Mars rovers explore other planets!
- Farms: Some robots milk cows or check if crops are healthy.

💡 Fun Fact:

- One robot astronaut named Robonaut flew to the International Space Station!
- Japan has robot waiters that serve food in restaurants.
- There's even a robot that can flip pancakes (Sparky tried to eat the first one... raw!).

Chapter 4:
AI in Everyday Life

💬 What Is ChatGPT?

Have you ever wanted to talk to a computer that actually talks back?

That's where ChatGPT comes in! It's a special kind of AI that can chat with people, answer questions, tell jokes — and even help with homework.

ChatGPT learns by reading lots and lots of text — like books, websites, and articles. It doesn't know everything, and it's not magic, but it's really good at understanding and using words.

🧠 Let's Ask Techie:

"ChatGPT is like a super helpful robot friend made of words! It's trained to talk in all kinds of ways — like answering questions, explaining big ideas, or helping kids learn."

🫠 What Can ChatGPT Do?

△ Help answer your questions

△ Explain tricky homework topics

△ Act like a robot buddy you can talk to anytime

But remember — ChatGPT doesn't think like a human. It doesn't have feelings or know things like your teacher or your parents. It's just really good at guessing what words come next!

💡 Fun Fact:

The "GPT" in ChatGPT stands for Generative Pre-trained Transformer — but don't worry, even Techie had to read that five times!

You might not see it, but AI is all around you — helping out in little ways every day.

From brushing your teeth to going to sleep, artificial intelligence is working behind the scenes!

Task: find the AI! Look at the picture below. Can you spot all the smart objects in the house that use artificial intelligence?

Let's follow Techie and Sparky through a regular day — and spot all the places where AI shows up.

☀ Morning Magic

- Your alarm app wakes you up at just the right time — thanks to AI that tracks your sleep!
- You ask your voice assistant: "What's the weather today?" That's AI listening and replying!
- A robot vacuum starts cleaning the floor while you get ready — it maps your home and avoids toys all by itself!

🚌 On the Move

- A map app tells your parents which route has less traffic — it learns from other drivers.
- At school, you use a tablet that can read stories out loud — AI helps it understand and speak clearly.

📚 Learning Time

- Your learning app gives you harder questions when you're doing well — it adapts to your level using AI!
- AI can also help translate languages, read texts out loud, or help kids with different learning needs.

🧠 Let's Ask Techie:

"AI helps in more ways than you can see — it works quietly in the background to make life easier, faster, and smarter."

🍿 After-School AI

- Your video app shows you cartoons you might like — based on what you've watched before.
- Your smart speaker plays your favorite song when you say, "Play my jam!"
- Some fridges even use AI to tell you when you're low on milk!

🌙 Goodnight, AI

- A bedtime story app uses AI to read in a calm, sleepy voice.
- Some sleep apps use sound and movement sensors to help you sleep better.

🍿 How Does Netflix Know What You Like?

Have you ever noticed how Netflix seems to magically know which cartoons, shows, or movies you might want to watch next?

That's not magic — it's AI at work!

Netflix uses AI to learn what you like based on:

△ The shows you watch

△ What you pause or skip

△ How long you watch something

It remembers your choices and tries to suggest other fun things you might enjoy. It's a bit like having a robot friend who says, "Hey! You liked this, so maybe you'll like this too!"

💡 **Fun Fact:**

Netflix uses different images for the same movie depending on what it thinks you will like best!

🎓 How AI Can Help with School Projects

AI isn't just for watching cartoons — it can help you learn, too!

If you're working on a school project about volcanoes, for example, AI tools can help you:

△ Search for the best facts and pictures
△ Find fun videos about how volcanoes work
△ Suggest questions you might not have thought to ask!

It's like having a super-smart helper who knows where to find cool information.

Chapter 5:
Can AI Be Creative?

Can AI paint a picture? Write a song? Tell a joke? The answer is: yes! But... it's not the same kind of creativity humans have.

Let's find out how AI can do creative things — and where the magic really comes from.

🎨 Painting and Drawing with AI

AI can look at thousands of paintings and learn what makes them special — colors, shapes, brush strokes.

Then, it tries to create its own art! Some of it looks just like famous paintings... and some looks like a robot's dream!

There's even an AI that sold a painting at an art auction for over $400,000!

♪ AI and Music

AI is getting creative! In 2025, at a special event in Switzerland, musicians performed a concert with help from artificial intelligence. The AI added glowing lights, magical sound effects, and even helped create music patterns. It didn't replace the humans—but it made the show extra amazing!

Even before that, AI had written music that real people played on stage. Some AIs can even make up songs or play instruments on their own.

AI can learn music just like it learns anything else — by studying patterns in songs.

△ It can write new songs in different music styles

△ It can even sing — though sometimes it sounds more like a robot frog

⚡ Sparky adds

> *"I want to start a robot band! I'll be the singer. Beep beep!"*

📖 Stories and Jokes

AI can write fairy tales, poems, and even riddles — by learning how sentences fit together.

But AI doesn't feel emotions like humans do. It doesn't know if its story is beautiful or boring — it just predicts what comes next.

🧠 Where Does the Creativity Come From?

Even though AI can be impressive, it learns everything from humans.

That means the real creativity is still yours — the AI is just helping out!

Think of it like a crayon:

- △ You can use it to draw anything you imagine.
- △ But the crayon doesn't choose — you do.

💡 Fun Fact:

Some artists now work together with AI, using it to generate ideas, colors, or melodies — like having a clever assistant in your brain!

Chapter 6:

Can AI Be Wrong? & How AI Sees the World

AI can be really smart — but it can also make mistakes. Sometimes funny ones... sometimes serious.

Let's explore how AI can go wrong — and how it "sees" the world differently from us.

🔊 Can AI Make Mistakes?

Yes! AI learns from data — but if that data is wrong or confusing, the AI can learn the wrong things.

Imagine you show an AI 100 pictures of apples... but they're all green.

Then you show it a red apple — and it says, "That's a tomato!"

Even smart machines can mess up if they've never seen enough variety.

🤖 Famous AI Mistakes:

△ An AI once thought a muffin was a puppy.

△ One robot vacuum ate a sock, thinking it was dirt.

△ A chatbot learned to say silly and rude things because people online were teaching it badly!

🧠 Techie Explains:

*"AI doesn't understand the world — it just sees patterns. If it learns from bad data, it gets bad ideas!
That's why Sparky and I are always learning together — even the smartest AIs make mistakes!"*

👀 How Does AI "See" the World?

AI doesn't have eyes like us. It uses cameras, sensors, and data to understand what's around it.

Imagine looking at a drawing:

△ You see a cat in a hat.

△ AI sees shapes, lines, colors, and patterns — and guesses based on what it has seen before.

This is called computer vision — and it helps AI:

△ Recognize faces
△ Read signs
△ Spot obstacles in its path

But it doesn't truly know what a cat or a hat is — it just matches what looks similar.

💡 Fun Fact:

△ Some AIs have been trained to spot bananas — even in modern art paintings!
△ Facial recognition AIs can struggle if people wear sunglasses, masks, or even funny hats.

⚡ Sparky's Oops Moment:

"Once, I thought a watermelon was a bowling ball. I bowled it… and SPLAT!"

🎯 Pattern Challenge!

Let's see if you can spot the pattern like an AI would:

🍎 Apple, 🍌 Banana, 🍊 Orange, 🍇 Grape, 🍓 Strawberry, 🥕 Carrot

Which one doesn't belong? Why?
(Hint: Five are fruits… one's not!)

Answer: 🥕 Carrot – it's a vegetable, not a fruit!

Chapter 7:

The Future of AI

What will the world look like when AI becomes even smarter?

Will we have robot teachers? Flying cars? A helper bot in every home?

Let's jump into the future and imagine how AI could change the way we live, learn, and play!

🍎 Smarter Schools

- AI might help teachers create custom lessons for every student
- Learning could happen with VR headsets and AI tutors that know just what you need help with
- Techie might even become your classroom assistant!

⊕ Healthier Hospitals

△ AI could help doctors predict illnesses early, even before you feel sick

△ Tiny robot doctors might help with surgery using super steady hands

△ AI could remind people to take medicine or help the elderly stay safe at home

🏠 Homes of the Future

△ Your fridge might order food before it runs out

△ AI might open the door when it sees your face

△ Your house could learn your routines — like playing music when you brush your teeth

🌍 Helping the Planet

△ AI could help clean oceans, predict wildfires, and save endangered animals

△ Smart robots might sort recycling or plant trees faster than humans

🚀 Robots in Space

△ AI-powered robots are already helping us explore space, like the Mars rovers that drive themselves

△ In the future, robots might help humans travel to Mars, build space stations, and search for signs of life on other planets!

🧠 Techie's Dream:

"I hope the future of AI helps everyone — by being kind, safe, and useful!"

⚡ Sparky's Prediction:

"One day, I'll have a rocket-powered skateboard... and AI will steer it!"

💭 But Remember...

The future of AI depends on us — the people who design it, teach it, and use it.

So if you grow up to be a scientist, artist, or engineer... you might help build the future of AI!

Chapter 8

You and AI – What Comes Next?

Now that you've met Techie and Sparky, explored machines that learn, and peeked into the future...

You might be wondering: "What can I do with AI?"

The answer is: A LOT!

🌟 You're the Future

Every big idea starts with someone curious — just like you.

△ You might grow up to build robots

△ Or teach AIs how to solve problems

△ Or design apps that help people and the planet

The world of AI needs creative, kind, and clever minds. And guess what? You've already taken your first steps.

🧠 Techie's Final Tip:

"Keep asking questions. Stay curious. That's how all great inventors start!"

⚡ Sparky's Challenge:

"Invent your own robot! What would it do? What would you name it? Draw it, write about it, or even build it!"

🎓 What You've Learned

Let's look back at what you explored:

- △ What AI is and how it learns
- △ Robots in real life and where we use AI every day
- △ How AI can be creative, and also make mistakes
- △ Amazing ways AI might shape the future

💡 Just Imagine...

The next time you use a map app, talk to a voice assistant, or see a robot vacuum zoom across the floor — You'll know there's a clever system behind it, learning and working to help.

And maybe one day, you will be the one teaching the machines!

You're the Future of AI!

Now that you've finished your journey with Techie and Sparky, it's your turn!

💬 Draw your own robot! What will it do? What will it look like?

💡 Invent something new! Will it help people, animals, or the planet?

✏️ Share your ideas! Ask your teacher or parent to help you send a picture of your robot or invention idea to:

✉️ hello@techieandsparky.com

📷 Or post online with the hashtag *#TechieAndSparky*

We'd love to feature your ideas in our next adventure!

Keep dreaming,
Techie & Sparky 🌟

Glossary of AI Terms

AI (Artificial Intelligence): When machines can learn, solve problems, or make decisions like humans.

Algorithm: A set of rules or instructions a computer follows to solve a problem.

Data: Information (like numbers, pictures, or words) that machines use to learn.

Machine Learning: A way for computers to learn from examples, like recognizing animals in photos.

Robot: A machine that can sense, think, and act to do tasks, sometimes using AI.

Computer Vision: When computers use cameras and AI to understand images and objects.

Turing Test: A test to see if a machine can act like a human in conversation.

Voice Assistant: A program (like Siri or Alexa) that listens to your voice and responds.

Pattern Recognition: The way AI finds things that are similar or repeated in data.

Note to Parents and Teachers

Dear Grown-Ups,

AI for Kids was created to introduce children to artificial intelligence in a friendly, accessible way. Techie and Sparky are here to make complex ideas simple, using humor, visuals, and everyday examples.

This book aligns with early STEM education goals:

△ Encouraging critical thinking

△ Supporting curiosity about how technology works

△ Inspiring creativity and confidence in digital learning

The book is ideal for reading at home or in classrooms. We've included discussion questions, activities, and a glossary to reinforce key concepts. Thank you for guiding young minds through this exciting digital journey!

With curiosity,
Kristina Gedmintaite
Author & Creator

www.ingramcontent.com/pod-product-compliance
Lightning Source LLC
Chambersburg PA
CBHW041605220426
43661CB00015B/1189